T.

Church Times Study Guide

The Same But Different

The Synoptic Gospels

John Holdsworth

CANTERBURY
PRESS
Norwich

First published in 2006 by the Canterbury Press Norwich
(a publishing imprint of Hymns Ancient & Modern Limited,
a registered charity)
St Mary's Works, St Mary's Plain,
Norwich, Norfolk NR3 3BH

www.scm-canterburypress.co.uk

British Library Cataloguing in Publication data

A catalogue record for this book is available
from the British Library

ISBN 1–85311–701–3/978–1–85311–701–5

Typeset by Regent Typesetting, London
Printed and bound by
Gallpen Colour Print, Norwich

Contents

Introduction

Problem? What Problem?

If you were to introduce the Christian scriptures to a friend who knew nothing about them, what would you choose for starters? The probable answer is, one of the Gospels. In a world of complication here is a shaft of accessible simplicity. To read the Gospels, it seems, we don't have to understand all the complicated vocabulary of Paul in his letters, we don't have to enter the visionary world of Revelation, we don't have to understand a load of obscure ancient history. Here are familiar and readable stories about Jesus, the focus of our faith. Read them, be touched and believe. It's pretty straightforward.

But let's suppose for a moment that this were a slightly awkward friend, used to reading adult books with no pictures in, and happy to discuss the issues they raise. She might ask:

- What exactly is it that I'm reading? Is it a novel, a memoir, a biography, or a piece of historical reportage?
- What can I compare it with? Are there any non-Christian Gospels, for example? How can I see what is distinctive about this way of writing?
- Why are there four of them, and why are three so very similar and one so very different?
- What kind of reaction am I meant to have to this writing? Is it a discussion document or a piece of propaganda? Or am I meant to be moved by it in some way? Why was it written?

Reflection

Suppose you did do as this opening paragraph suggests, and your friend did in fact ask: 'What are you giving me? How should I read this?' what would you say? It may be worth returning to this question at the end of the study to see if your answer has changed.

The possible answers to those questions reveal further mysteries.

- The Gospels are not memoirs because they're not written in the first person. They are not biographies in the usual sense because they do not describe the whole of Jesus' life. Only two of them describe his birth. One of them describes a brief incident in his childhood. None of them takes any further interest in him at all until he is well into middle age (by the standards of the time). All of them spend a disproportionate amount of time describing the events of just one week. The writing is not as dispassionate and objective as pure historical reportage might demand. So the answer seems to be: none of the above.
- The word 'Gospel' means good news, and is a specifically Christian invention. There are no non-Christian Gospels and attempts to find comparable literary genres have been relatively unconvincing, though there are some possible links between some of the writings and other contemporary literature. Not much of an answer there then.
- If we look in any detail at the third question we enter a discussion that has been occupying scholars for over a century of fairly intense debate. Matthew, Mark and Luke are similar to each other but quite different from John. In fact it is possible to construct a synopsis of the first three Gospels to show where they coincide; hence they have come to be known as the 'synoptic Gospels'. But what is the relationship between them? Was one of them available to the authors of the others, or did they write independently. (Surely not, when you consider how close the similarities are.) If they were writing from sources, does that mean

they were not simply jotting down things they remembered from their own experience? (Yes it does.)

- And that all adds weight to the question: why did they write at all? Were the later writers trying to improve on the work of their predecessors, or were they writing for different contexts and audiences? If so, what can we know about all that, and does it matter? And what result did they expect their work to have? Why am I reading it now?
- And underlying all of this is the question: if these writers did have a serious motive, then how am I to recognize that? What is the point at which fact merges with opinion, where argument is combined with narrative? How is the writer trying to persuade me? And ultimately, is the urgency with which all this was treated in the early church recognizable in our own situation? Does it still matter whether I'm persuaded or not about these issues?

This is a study guide for those who have the kind of curiosity that wants to know as much as possible about how to read the Gospels intelligently. This is too short a study to include all four Gospels so we shall confine ourselves more or less to the first three – the synoptic Gospels – and we shall try to see how we can get more from reading the Gospels by looking at the work of scholars from the last hundred years or so.

- This is first of all a work of unravelling. What were the original sources of the Gospels? Traditionally this has been known as *source criticism*.
- Then it's a detective job, to see how those sources were combined, and in what circumstances. Traditionally this has been known as *form criticism*.
- Then it's an observation and reconstruction job, to notice the differences between the Gospels more carefully, and to see if we can imagine what each Gospel was trying to achieve. Traditionally this has been known as *redaction criticism*.
- Finally it's a job of reflection, to see what we can learn in our own circumstances from this whole enterprise. This is a task of *exegesis and practical theology.*

Exercise

It's sometimes a bit of a surprise to learn that the differences between the Gospels might matter. We're used to things like nativity plays and passion plays that skirt over the differences. Just to make a start on noticing difference, you might like to read Matthew 1.18—2.23, and then compare it with Luke 1.26–38, and 2.1–20. These are both accounts of the birth of Jesus. Do they have anything in common? Make a list of the things that only occur in one account.

You could follow that up by reading Mark 14.53–65; 15.1–15, and compare that with Luke 22.66—23.1–25. The differences here are more subtle, but still very interesting. You could begin to notice them by asking questions like:

What is the political agenda of each writer?
Where does each writer want the blame to lie for this?
What words does each writer put into the mouth of Jesus? Do the differences matter?
Which is the longer account and why is it longer?

The study guide will follow this plan. Chapter 1 will describe the problem of the synoptic Gospels as scholars have seen it, through the stages of source and form criticism above. Chapter 2 will look at what redaction and literary criticism have added, to bring us right up to date. Chapter 3 will look at what all this means for our understanding of the Gospels, with exercises to test our own skills. A brief final section will point us in the direction of further reading and resources.

1

A Good Night Out

Exercise

Read Matthew 9.9–13; Mark 2.13–17; Luke 5.27–32. If it's possible to copy those passages so that you can see them side by side so much the better. These three accounts are clearly very similar. The similarities are too close to be accidental, and yet there are differences as well. See how many you can spot. At this stage they might not seem very significant but later you might return to this exercise and see more significance in them. Use a Bible such as RSV or REB that translates the text closely to get maximum benefit. One other thing you might notice is that each of the writers introduces this account at a completely different place in his Gospel. For Mark, it's right at the beginning, but for Matthew it doesn't appear until Chapter 9.

The problem that scholars of the synoptic Gospels have had to deal with is: why are these Gospels so similar and yet different? Similarities so close suggest something more than differences between individual memories. They suggest sources. The first question we might ask is then, was one of these Gospels an original source for the other two? Which one was first? Despite the fact that Matthew is placed first in our Bibles, the consensus is that Mark was first for these reasons.

- Of Mark's 661 verses, 600 occur in Matthew. It's easier to see that Matthew would have expanded on Mark than that Mark would have shortened Matthew.

- Matthew and Luke never agree when they diverge from Mark.
- Mark contains lots of picturesque detail. If there was a period when these sources were transmitted orally, by word of mouth, that's the kind of detail which might be included, and perhaps omitted by a later writer.
- Matthew and Luke follow Mark's order. This is a point we can easily miss if we're used to the Gospels. John's Gospel does not follow the same order, even when it includes the same or similar incidents. For example, in the synoptic Gospels the cleansing of the Temple comes at the end of Jesus' life, as he enters Jerusalem for the last time, whereas in John it occurs right at the beginning.

Exercise

Just to get the flavour of the third point above, read Mark 6.30–44, and compare it with Matthew 14.13–21 which is only about half as long. Notice the differences. What would make more sense to you – that Mark had expanded on Matthew or that Matthew had edited Mark?

So we imagine Matthew and Luke sitting down with a copy of Mark in front of them and setting out to write their Gospels. Matthew uses virtually all of Mark apart from some of what he seems to conclude is irrelevant detail. Luke uses about half of Mark. What else do they include? It's worth pointing out that any sources either of them relied on are likely to have been oral. Some scholars think that written collections of some kinds were circulating prior to the production of the Gospels, but there was probably a long oral phase in any case. The Gospel of Mark is generally dated around the first half of the 60s – around thirty years, or a whole generation or more, after the first Easter. In fact that may have been a reason why Gospels began to be written – because the personal oral link was dying out. But how can we unravel any further sources?

One clue is that there is a body of material that is common to Matthew and Luke, but which does not appear in Mark. There are between 200 and 250 verses of this material, which include some very familiar scenes and sayings. They include, for example, the temptation of Jesus, the great sermon, and the missionary charge to the apostles. Most of the material is in the form of memorable sayings rather than narrative, and they include some parables such as the parable of the talents. Because the initial work on this material 150 years ago was by German scholars, they used German terms to describe it. Consequently, this body of common material is known by the first letter of a German word, Q.

But even if we think of Matthew and Luke using both Mark and Q as sources, that does not exhaust all the material they contain. There is some material that only appears in Matthew. We have, for example, already seen that the birth of Jesus falls into that category. Other familiar passages only in Matthew include his account of the resurrection in Chapter 28 and the parable of the sheep and the goats in Chapter 25. Also he includes a lot of quotations from the Old Testament which are peculiar to him, and he includes a lot of teaching material (which he groups together into five teaching blocks) which the others do not. This material is labelled, conveniently, 'special M'.

As you might imagine, then, there is also a 'special L' category for material which only appears in Luke, such as his birth narratives, parables such as the prodigal son or the good Samaritan, and accounts such as that of the ten lepers in Chapter 17.

So source criticism produces the conclusion that there are four sources for the Gospels: Mark, Q, special M and special L. In its day this was controversial scholarship, because it contradicted the idea that the Gospels were eye-witness accounts written by the apostles themselves. The authors of the Gospels were seen rather as editors of material, which had been handed on for a considerable period through a process of oral tradition.

The next stage in the detective process, which covered a considerable part of the twentieth century, was to focus attention rather more on what happened to these stories, sayings and other material that we now find in the Gospels, from their origin to the point at which they were incorporated into the Gospels by the authors. The kinds of question which now interested scholars were:

- How was the material kept in the memory? Were there, for example, particular stories related to particular localities where Jesus had been? Did stories of a particular kind circulate as some kind of collection?
- Were there first editions which brought together some of the material in a collected form? For example, might it have been that the passion narrative, the account of Jesus' trial and crucifixion, took shape and circulated independently?
- Why were the stories and sayings remembered at all? Were they remembered mostly by the Church and used in some early form of preaching, for example? Or might the Church have used something like the passion narrative as a framework for something along the lines of an early Eucharist as churches do today? Again, might some of the material have been remembered in more secular settings?
- Is it in fact possible to classify the material in some way that would enable answers to these kinds of question? Could we say, well this kind of material was remembered by this group for this reason, but this other kind of material was remembered in a different way by different people?

And again, very controversially, this kind of questioning led to questions about how original these sources really were. If a saying or story of Jesus, or about Jesus, has been repeated many times over many years, or if it has been designed for some specific use in the Church, might it not be the case that the original material has been added to, or adapted, or interpreted in a way which makes it difficult to say with certainty that any particular 'saying of Jesus' is actually traceable back to him? The longer the period of oral transmission, and the more creative role we might give to the community of faith during this period, the more those kinds of question are raised. Some scholars believed, over 100 years ago, that it was well nigh impossible to authenticate the Gospel material back to Jesus himself, or that it was well nigh impossible to write an accurate history of his life. They said that what we have in the Gospels is rather a presentation of the significance of Jesus, as the early Church understood it and wanted to express it in its own missionary endeavour.

One example of the kind of work these so-called form critics (again from a German term) were doing actually comes from John's Gospel, Chapter 2. This is the familiar story of the marriage at Cana, where Jesus turns water into wine. According to one French scholar this was based on the kind of story that circulated about Jesus in secular circles. In fact he thinks it was based on a kind of after-dinner story. In its original form it was about how Jesus, well known for his notorious habits of eating and drinking with prostitutes and sinners, had been invited (with the boys) to a wedding for a good old three-day event of merrymaking – a good night out. At some point in the proceedings his mother was also present and tells him it's time to go home. But he will have none of it. He says something along the lines of: 'What on earth are you talking about, woman? My hour has not yet come.' In other words, 'I'm not ready to go home yet, just because the wine's run out.' And he performs his miracle and keeps on going. All good stuff for a secular after-dinner occasion for the uncommitted who might have heard of this Jesus. In the French scholar's view the author of the Gospel of John picked this story up and used it in his Gospel, but completely changed its meaning – a good communication technique. In the Gospel version, when Jesus says, 'My hour has not yet come,' he is seen to refer to his death and resurrection, and the image of the wine is related to the 'new wine' theme we are familiar with from elsewhere.

That's an interesting theory, though nothing more than that. It does however point to the extent to which form critics were moving in the direction of seeing the Gospel authors as quite sophisticated editors. That thrust of their work was taken up and developed by others, as we shall see in the next section. They are remembered mostly now for their detailed responses to the bullet point questions above – their attempt to get a handle on how the oral material became part of the Gospels.

They attempted this using a three-stage process. The *first stage* was to classify material by genre or, to use the German word, *Gattung*. Scholars read the Gospels closely and tried to identify similar ways of writing.

Exercise

Read Mark 2.23–8; Mark 3.31–5; Luke 14.1–6. Do you see any similarities in the style of these three accounts? Are they sufficiently similar to constitute a particular type of writing, do you think? Now read on.

One example of a genre they reckoned to have found is given various names, but we shall call them pronouncement stories. All three accounts in our exercise above are said to be examples of this genre. It is defined as having three elements. Each begins by briefly setting the scene. Then there is a (brief) description of some action. Finally there is a significant pronouncement by Jesus himself of the kind that seems to be pretty final as far as that issue is concerned.

Look again at the examples above. Do you recognize this pattern in the texts?

The *second stage* was to ask how and why were these kinds of pronouncement story remembered? What was the situation in real life (or using the German term, *Sitz im Leben*), which maintained and treasured and developed this particular kind of story? The answer to that had a bearing on the *third stage*, which was to ask: How historically reliable is this text? Is it more or less likely, once we can identify how it was transmitted, that the Church has had some creative role in these stories? This is clearly much more of an art than a science, and conclusions vary greatly about all aspects of the process. There is some disagreement (though not much) about the identification of the genres. There is far more disagreement about the ascription of a *Sitz im Leben*, and an almost infinite set of possibilities when we come to assessing the historicity (that is the historicalness) of the material.

So, to take our examples: some writers think they had their main use in situations of conflict between the Church and their opponents. This would account for the strong pronouncement style of Jesus' utterance. Some think they were used in preaching. Some think they were used for instructing new converts. There is fairly widespread agreement that this material is early, though the Church may well have had a creative role of some sort in presenting it in particular contexts.

Reflection

Perhaps you can think of situations where this happens nowadays. Think of a familiar Gospel story. Then consider how the telling of the story differs if used in say,

'
- a children's address
- a prayer
- a hymn
- a sermon to adults

What kind of thing is added or omitted, in your experience?

Other classifications include miracle stories, sayings of Jesus, and what some scholars call legends or stories about Jesus.

Reflection

Think of the transmission of miracle stories. Was this more likely to be in secular or religious settings, do you think? How would this affect your view of their reliability?

The main results of form criticism are then that:

- the Gospels are not eye-witness accounts;
- the Gospels are crafted creations, not arbitrary collections;
- they are shaped by the needs of the community, such as conflict, teaching, preaching;
- Gospels have an agenda.

The next stage in the critical adventure is in part a development of form criticism and particularly the idea that the context of each Gospel is important for understanding it. In part also it is a reaction to some of the negative results of form criticism, and especially the way it focuses attention on little bits of the text. It's possible to get so hung up on how tiny fragments of text were transmitted that we lose sight of the finished article, and perhaps even worse, lose interest in it. The stage is then set for *redaction criticism*.

2

Riding the Storm

Redaction is one more technical term which comes from a German original. What it means is that we are encouraged to look at the final edition (also known as a redaction) of the text, rather than concentrating on how that final edition came into being. The kinds of question in which this stage in the detective process is interested are:

- What was the motivation behind each of the Gospels? Why was each of them written at the time it was and in the way it was?
- How creative was the author? How did he use his sources to craft this final product?
- How individual is each Gospel? Are the differences between Gospels noteworthy?

To the extent that this way of approaching the text is a development from source and form criticism, it works with their assumptions and conclusions: particularly that Mark is the first Gospel, and that Mark was a source for Matthew and Luke. It also works from the base that the authors are not scissors-and-paste editors, putting the material together in a haphazard way, but that there is a pattern and purpose to their work.

What exactly are we talking about when we describe these people as editors with sources? Well, one very obvious way of demonstrating the creative difference between the authors is to look at material whose original source was Mark. We can see how Matthew uses this material, and we can compare that with the way Luke uses it. That in turn may help to throw light on what is distinctive about Mark's use of it. Also, we can look at material that is obviously common to Matthew and Luke from the Q tradition, and yet is used subtly differently by each author.

What kind of thing are we looking for when we talk about 'difference' and 'editing?' Here are some examples which you can look at yourself.

Exercise

Look at the following passages from Mark, and compare them with the recycled version in Matthew as suggested. What do you think has changed?

Mark 6.45–52 – compare with Matthew 14.22–36.
Mark 10.18 – compare with Matthew 19.17.
Mark 2.1–12 – compare with Matthew 9.2–8

It may be that you have identified occasions when the editor's hand is evident by the way he *expands* on the material in Mark; or by the way he attempts to *rephrase* to avoid misunderstanding; or by the way he *omits* part of Mark's account to get rid of superfluous detail (as we have already seen). Other examples of editing are:

- Obvious editorial comment to explain what might not be obvious, as in Mark 7.3–4.
- Editorial seams and summaries, as in Mark 1.21–3; 3.11.
- Changing the order; for example, compare the different points where Matthew and Luke use the same verse: Matthew 23.37–9; Luke 13.34–5. This kind of change may seem small but can have wide consequences. To explore them fully means looking carefully at what precedes and follows the verses in each of their settings, and then making a good guess as to why they might differ. Again this is more of an art than a science. Different views are possible and this is part of what makes the whole thing so interesting – you can reach your own conclusions, rather than just having to accept what someone else has decreed.

The conclusion that redaction critics draw is well summed up by a German scholar of the late twentieth century, Günther Bornkamm, who has used the method widely. 'The Synoptic writers show – all three and each in his own special way – by their editing and construction, by their selection, inclusion and omission, and not least by what at first sight appears an insignificant, but on closer examination is seen to be a characteristic treatment of the traditional material, that they are by no means mere collectors and handers-on of the tradition, but are also interpreters of it.' (Bornkamm, Barth and Held, *Tradition and Interpretation in Matthew*, SCM Press, 1963, page 11)

What he means here by 'characteristic treatment' is, in effect, the second stage in the redaction criticism process. Having seen a number of examples of changes, the critic can see if they form some kind of pattern that might enable us to reach a wider conclusion about the author's beliefs and purposes. To take a hypothetical example: if we saw an author consistently altering any reference in a text to women, and changing it so that it referred instead to men, we might be justified in concluding that this was in fact part of the author's agenda. The final stage would be to ask: What situation in the life of the Church, what kind of context might have called for this kind of writing? And further, what does this tell us about the actual history of the community being addressed?

A famous essay by Bornkamm compares the stilling of the storm in Mark and Matthew, and reaches conclusions based on the way Matthew has used his source, which are then compared to other examples to reach conclusions about Matthew's general theological perspective. This is such a good example of the method at work that you might like to read the two passages concerned and follow his argument.

Exercise

Read Mark 4.35–41 and Matthew 8.23–7. This is a familiar story and it may well be that you have never considered that any differences between Gospels was in any way significant. But now read it closely and make a list of all the differences you can see between these two texts. You might like to read a little more widely to compare the settings of each of the stories in their respective Gospels. Having made your own list you can compare it with that which Bornkamm found, below.

In Mark's Gospel the setting of this story is among other miracle stories in which Jesus demonstrates his power. It is immediately followed by his demonstration of power to heal the mentally ill Legion, Jairus's daughter and the woman with the flow of blood which no one could cure. It is preceded by other healing miracles which show Jesus as a man of action. In Matthew's Gospel, the wider setting is a portion of the Gospel (bracketed by the repeated verse at 4.23 and 9.35) demonstrating Jesus as both teacher and doer. The immediate context is a question about discipleship, in which the word 'follow' appears especially significant. This is then linked to our story by that same word. Bornkamm thinks that this is important, indicating that actually this story is some kind of illustration about discipleship. This would mean that we should perhaps think of the journey in the boat as being in some sense the journey of the Church.

The next difference is not immediately apparent in English, but in Greek the word which Mark uses to describe the storm is the kind of word which meteorologists would use, and which gives us our word 'anemometer' – an instrument for measuring the force and ferocity of the wind. Matthew uses a different word, not *anemos*, but *seismos*. This word describes something much more cataclysmic and gives us the family of words with which to describe earthquakes. Such a word would be quite out of place to describe a storm on a lake. It does however occur once more in Matthew – at 28.2 where it marks, as a kind of fanfare, a resurrection appearance of Jesus. The suggestion is that, comparing these two, we see Matthew pointing to a resurrection experience for the early Church.

The next difference is just about recognizable in English, depending on the translation. What do the men say when they become frightened? In Mark they react like frightened men, and throw normal courtesy to the wind (so to speak), addressing Jesus in a very rough and ready way (note also Mark's detail of the cushion, which Matthew omits). In Matthew the address is quite different, and sounds almost like a prayer, especially in Greek: *Kyrie, sôson*, which for those who are used to saying 'Kyrie eleison' in church is similar enough to be suggestive. Bornkamm identifies this as the prayer of the Church as it hits turbulent times – 'Lord, save'.

The next interesting difference is when Jesus acts and when he speaks. In Mark he does what you would expect a miracle worker to do in a situation of crisis. He stills the storm, then enters discussion with the disciples about their lack of faith. In Matthew the whole thing seems more artificial. He has the discussion about faith before he stills the storm In other words the word of Jesus to the Church is an admonition to faith in the midst of the storm.

In Mark's version, finally, it is the disciples who confirm what has happened. In Matthew it is 'men', a term which does not refer to the disciples. Rather, says Bornkamm, it is those who are reached through the preaching of the Church. Whereas Mark had received this story in the tradition and used it for one purpose – to show Jesus as a mighty miracle worker perhaps – Matthew has taken it and given it a completely different purpose and meaning. For him, in Bornkamm's view, this is a story to demonstrate the danger and glory of discipleship, and is addressed to a completely different Church context. This editing example can then be compared with others to see if a theme emerges, and many scholars would agree that one of the characteristic themes of this Gospel is Matthew's interest in the Church (of which more below, Chapter 3).

Redaction criticism has helped us in these ways:

- It has concentrated our attention on the final edition and helped us have a more holistic view of each Gospel.
- It has opened up a new appreciation of the creative individuality of each of the synoptic Gospel writers.
- It has led to a new interest in and emphasis on the context of each Gospel, asking questions about what it was in that context that called for the Gospel to be written. That, in turn, has led to a new appreciation of the diversity of the approaches of New Testament writers. Why did Matthew (or whoever) write Matthew when Mark was clearly available to him, and presumably to his community? In what ways was it not adequate?
- The progression of Gospel writing has helped us to see something of the development of theological thinking in the early Church.

Those who have reservations about this method might say:

- It appears more definitive and historically trustworthy than it actually is, because it is all based on the four source theory, which is itself a hypothesis.
- It assumes that each Gospel was written for a single community, and focuses attention on that community whose existence is again essentially a hypothesis.
- It encourages the view that material was adapted to community use, and that the Church played a creative role in adding to the tradition; and discourages the view that a body of original material was presented with slight differences to different audiences.

Developments in Gospel reading during the past 25 years or so have in part been a development of what redaction criticism achieved, and in part a reaction against it. Scholars have certainly taken the idea of studying the final complete text seriously but have moved away from too much emphasis on the historical context of the writing. In fact they've come to study it not so much as one would study documents from history, but rather more in the way one would study works of literature. As one scholar put it, 'If the evangelists are authors, then they must be studied as other authors are studied.'

This so-called *literary criticism* is at a relatively early stage, but it's worth bearing in mind the difference it makes to the way we read texts. One important difference is that we are more concerned about the effect the work has on us in the present than we are with how it sounded to the first people who heard it – and that is a big difference, because there are different assumptions in each case about how you discern the meaning of the text. If it's to do with the past then you need to know a lot about the past, and a lot of your work will be 'unearthing' work which will rely on a particular kind of expert. If it's to do with what it does to you in the present, then we are more concerned about the skill of the author in getting us to see his point of view and about how the author uses various kinds of communication technique. This can mean using a different kind of expert who can tell us all about irony, rhetoric, narrative description, character development and plot. But it can also mean dispensing with experts altogether. Sisters and brothers can do it for themselves.

It's not just because it's a bit subversive that some people are cautious with this approach. It's fairly new, and new things always take a while to catch on. But some people find it difficult to apply methods used mostly in fiction to something that we want to believe has a basis in fact. And that is especially true when we are dealing with alleged facts about the life of Jesus. Also, we've got used to the idea that truth, in a Christian setting, means subscribing to commonly accepted traditions that are handed down, and around which there is some definitive boundary. If the text can mean whatever you want it to mean, that is threatened. Advocates of the literary approach would claim that this is a gross oversimplification, and say that we do actually, for the most part, read the Gospels as literature in any case, and that to do the further work on the literary skills of the author opens up new avenues, and provides checks on insights already claimed.

3

Vive la différence

So, with the Gospels 'unravelled' in the way they have been during the last 150 years we have reached the point where the most intelligent and interesting way of reading or hearing the Gospels appears to be one which

- discerns the particular style and emphasis of each individual Gospel writer, so that you say to yourself, 'that sounds like Luke to me', and so on;
- focuses attention on the community for whom the Gospel is created (and that can lead to further historical and sociological research, as well as to what the text tells us about the community's beliefs);
- prompts us to think about how the author as a creative author is attempting to tell his story, what he wants us to believe, and how he is achieving that.

Let's then look at one passage from each Gospel which could be said to be typical of the style and concerns of that author, to help us in our reading. We must bear in mind that these are only illustrations of some of the differences and characteristics. No one passage can capture every concern, but here are some that might give a flavour and prompt you to dig further.

Exercise

To start with Matthew, read chapter 18.1–20. If you read this in a Bible with a cross-reference system you will see that this passage is a gathering together of bits and pieces from all over the other Gospels, together with some material that is special M, and only in Matthew. This gathering of teaching material into blocks is a feature of Matthew. Now read the passage carefully and see if you can find evidence of each of the following:

- a didactic, teaching style, that lays down the law in a definite way;
- lurid and dramatic hyperbole;
- a mood which is urgent about the decisions you make now really mattering;
- an interest in accountability and judgement;
- a focus on the life of the church and how it should operate;
- allied to this, a focus on leadership and authority.

You might like to look at other passages in Matthew and compare your findings, or look at how other Gospel writers use similar material.

Now let's have a look at a passage from Mark.

Read Mark 8.22—9.1

This is a section that both Matthew and Luke use and you might want to look at their use of it. But remember, just because Mark was first doesn't mean he has no theology, or special characteristics. See if you can find evidence for:

- Mark's favourite ways of describing Jesus;
- a focus on the passion, and suffering of Jesus;
- an emphasis on true discipleship;
- a geographical interest which is not just centred on Jerusalem;
- the power of Jesus.

And finally, a passage from Luke.

Read Luke 10.25—11.4. Most of this section occurs only in Luke. Can you now identify some of its particular features? You will probably list these among others:

- an interest in foreigners and outsiders;
- a particular interest in the role of women;
- an interest in prayer;
- a focus on ordinary domestic life.

You might like to glance through other parts of Luke's Gospel to see if what you have found is duplicated there.

So, what might you tell your awkward friend now, if she asked of a Gospel, 'What's this and what am I supposed to do with it?'

4

Going Further

There are three kinds of book you might like to attempt if you've been interested so far.

- One is the kind that looks at a specific area of Gospel study, and which is informed by the kind of scholarship we've been talking about. Examples would be Jeffrey John's *The Meaning in the Miracles* (SCM-Canterbury Press, 2001), or from an earlier period, any of H. J. Richards' excellent series of What Really Happened books. One example would be H. J. Richards, *The First Easter: What Really Happened?* My edition is the Fount edition of 1980, but there are later reprints.
- A second possibility would be to get hold of a current teaching textbook on the Gospels. One that I have used and find accessible is David Wenham and Steve Walton, *Exploring the New Testament: Volume 1, Introducing the Gospels and Acts,* SPCK, 2001.
- A third option is to read a book that introduces the Gospels in the kind of way we have used here, but in greater depth and detail. One that more or less fits that bill is Clive Marsh and Steve Moyise, *Jesus and the Gospels, An Introduction* (Cassell Biblical Studies) Cassell, 1999.

Or you could just hope that the Church Times Study Guide series will come up with something else next month to interest and stimulate.